HOW MUCH DO YOU KNOW ABOUT?
Investigate, answer, draw, create and... learn!

Wanceulen Editorial
Wanceulen Notebook
© Wanceulen Editorial. S. L.
www.wanceulen.com y www.wanceuleneditorial.com
info@wanceuleneditorial.com
C/. Cristo del Desamparo y Abandono, 56 - 41006 Sevilla (España)
© Copyright: Wanceulen Editorial S.L.

How much do you know about...?

Investigate, answer, draw, create and... learn!

Instructions:

▸ Each page includes a Worksheet, with enough space for write information.

▸ Read the question from the header of each worksheet.

▸ Research the subject in books and on the internet

▸ Respond in the space reserved for it.

▸ Draw a situation that illustrates your response.

▸ In the last section of each Form include a personal opinion on the subject treated, and write some other alternative than what is established.

Have fun and learn! ...Knowledge is also fun.

Objectives:

▸ Improve your research capacity and develop the knowledge.

▸ Improve your creativity and develop your skills.

▸ Collect your own works and studies in the Notebooks "How much do you know of...?" By Wanceulen Notebook

▸ Its quality and careful presentation allows you to archive them in your Library as one more book.

■ *Read and answer the question.*

What are the origins of this sport?

■ *Investigate and write your answer.*

■ *Draw your answer.*

■ *Create and write your personal opinion, comments, variants, etc*

■ *Read and answer the question.*

What is the name of this sport in other languages? Name it in at least 5 other languages.

■ *Investigate and write your answer.*

■ *Draw your answer.*

■ *Create and write your personal opinion, comments, variants, etc*

Read and answer the question.

What does this sport consist of? How is the game developed?

Investigate and write your answer.

Draw your answer.

Create and write your personal opinion, comments, variants, etc

■ *Read and answer the question.*

How much is the official field of play? How much is the reduced official field of play for children?

■ *Investigate and write your answer.*

■ *Draw your answer.*

■ *Create and write your personal opinion, comments, variants, etc*

■ *Read and answer the question.*

What are the name of the lines, zones and areas and how much does each measure?

■ *Investigate and write your answer.*

■ *Draw your answer.*

■ *Create and write your personal opinion, comments, variants, etc*

■ *Read and answer the question.*

State the title of all rules of the game

■ *Investigate and write your answer.*

■ *Draw your answer.*

■ *Create and write your personal opinion, comments, variants, etc*

■ *Read and answer the question.*

What are the main rules of the game in your opinion? Define them.

■ *Investigate and write your answer.*

■ *Draw your answer.*

■ *Create and write your personal opinion, comments, variants, etc*

Read and answer the question.

How many players initially play on each team? How many substitute players can be on he bench? How many changes can be made?

Investigate and write your answer.

Draw your answer.

Create and write your personal opinion, comments, variants, etc

■ Read and answer the question.

With how many minimum players must a team count to be able to play a match?

■ Investigate and write your answer.

■ Draw your answer.

■ Create and write your personal opinion, comments, variants, etc

■ *Read and answer the question.*

How long does a match last? How many periods of play and rest does a match have and how long do they last?

■ *Investigate and write your answer.*

■ *Draw your answer.*

■ *Create and write your personal opinion, comments, variants, etc*

■ *Read and answer the question.*

What are the most important faults that can punish a player during a match?

■ *Investigate and write your answer.*

■ *Draw your answer.*

■ *Create and write your personal opinion, comments, variants, etc*

■ *Read and answer the question.*

How can the non-statutory actions of players be sanctioned?

■ *Investigate and write your answer.*

■ *Draw your answer.*

■ *Create and write your personal opinion, comments, variants, etc*

■ *Read and answer the question.*

What elements, besides the body itself, are needed to play this sport? With what parts of the body can the ball be touched?

■ *Investigate and write your answer.*

■ *Draw your answer.*

■ *Create and write your personal opinion, comments, variants, etc*

■ *Read and answer the question.*

When is the Goal valid ?

■ *Investigate and write your answer.*

■ *Draw your answer.*

■ *Create and write your personal opinion, comments, variants, etc*

■ *Read and answer the question.*

What is the difference between tactics and technique?

■ *Investigate and write your answer.*

■ *Draw your answer.*

■ *Create and write your personal opinion, comments, variants, etc*

■ *Read and answer the question.*

Name all defensive technical actions

■ *Investigate and write your answer.*

■ *Draw your answer.*

■ *Create and write your personal opinion, comments, variants, etc*

■ *Read and answer the question.*

What are the 3 main defensive technical actions of the game in your opinion? Define them.

■ *Investigate and write your answer.*

■ *Draw your answer.*

■ *Create and write your personal opinion, comments, variants, etc*

■ *Read and answer the question.*

Name all offensive technical ball actions

■ *Investigate and write your answer.*

■ *Draw your answer.*

■ *Create and write your personal opinion, comments, variants, etc*

■ *Read and answer the question.*

What are the 3 main offensive technical actions of the game in your opinion? Define them.

■ *Investigate and write your answer.*

■ *Draw your answer.*

■ *Create and write your personal opinion, comments, variants, etc*

■ *Read and answer the question.*

Name all defensive tactical actions

■ *Investigate and write your answer.*

■ *Draw your answer.*

■ *Create and write your personal opinion, comments, variants, etc*

Read and answer the question.

What are the 3 main defensive tactical actions of the game in your opinion? Define them.

Investigate and write your answer.

Draw your answer.

Create and write your personal opinion, comments, variants, etc

■ *Read and answer the question.*

Name all offensive tactical ball actions

■ *Investigate and write your answer.*

■ *Draw your answer.*

■ *Create and write your personal opinion, comments, variants, etc*

Read and answer the question.

What are the 3 main offensive tactical actions of the game in your opinion? Define them.

Investigate and write your answer.

Draw your answer.

Create and write your personal opinion, comments, variants, etc

Read and answer the question.

Say how all technical offensive and defensive actions are named in Spanish.

Investigate and write your answer.

Draw your answer.

Create and write your personal opinion, comments, variants, etc

■ *Read and answer the question.*

Say how all tactical offensive and defensive actions are named in Spanish

■ *Investigate and write your answer.*

■ *Draw your answer.*

■ *Create and write your personal opinion, comments, variants, etc*

■ *Read and answer the question.*

Design an exercise to train a defensive action

■ *Investigate and write your answer.*

■ *Draw your answer.*

■ *Create and write your personal opinion, comments, variants, etc*

Read and answer the question.

Design an exercise to train an offensive action

Investigate and write your answer.

Draw your answer.

Create and write your personal opinion, comments, variants, etc

■ *Read and answer the question.*

What are the main strategy actions? Also name them in Spanish.

■ *Investigate and write your answer.*

■ *Draw your answer.*

■ *Create and write your personal opinion, comments, variants, etc*

■ *Read and answer the question.*

What are the most used gaming systems currently?

■ *Investigate and write your answer.*

■ *Draw your answer.*

■ *Create and write your personal opinion, comments, variants, etc*

■ *Read and answer the question.*

What are the specific positions or positions of the players? Also name them inSpanish.

■ *Investigate and write your answer.*

■ *Draw your answer.*

■ *Create and write your personal opinion, comments, variants, etc*

■ *Read and answer the question.*

What are the 3 main functions of each of the positions or positions?

■ *Investigate and write your answer.*

■ *Draw your answer.*

■ *Create and write your personal opinion, comments, variants, etc*

■ *Read and answer the question.*

What are the most important physical qualities?

■ *Investigate and write your answer.*

■ *Draw your answer.*

■ *Create and write your personal opinion, comments, variants, etc*

■ *Read and answer the question.*

What are the most important psychological qualities?

■ *Investigate and write your answer.*

■ *Draw your answer.*

■ *Create and write your personal opinion, comments, variants, etc*

■ *Read and answer the question.*

Say how all the physical qualities are named in Spanish, German and French.

■ *Investigate and write your answer.*

■ *Draw your answer.*

■ *Create and write your personal opinion, comments, variants, etc*

■ *Read and answer the question.*

Say how all the psychological qualities are named in Spanish, German and French.

■ *Investigate and write your answer.*

■ *Draw your answer.*

■ *Create and write your personal opinion, comments, variants, etc*

■ *Read and answer the question.*

What qualities are the most important for the game, the technical qualities, the tactical qualities, the physical qualities or the psychological qualities? Give reasons for your answer.

■ *Investigate and write your answer.*

■ *Draw your answer.*

■ *Create and write your personal opinion, comments, variants, etc*

■ *Read and answer the question.*

What are the main functions of coaches?

■ *Investigate and write your answer.*

■ *Draw your answer.*

■ *Create and write your personal opinion, comments, variants, etc*

■ *Read and answer the question.*
....
Who are the most important national coaches in history?

■ *Investigate and write your answer.*
....

■ *Draw your answer.*
....

■ *Create and write your personal opinion, comments, variants, etc*
....

■ *Read and answer the question.*

Who are the most important international coaches in history?

■ *Investigate and write your answer.*

■ *Draw your answer.*

■ *Create and write your personal opinion, comments, variants, etc*

■ *Read and answer the question.*

Who are the most important national coaches currently?

■ *Investigate and write your answer.*

■ *Draw your answer.*

■ *Create and write your personal opinion, comments, variants, etc*

Read and answer the question.

Who are the most important international coaches currently?

Investigate and write your answer.

Draw your answer.

Create and write your personal opinion, comments, variants, etc

■ *Read and answer the question.*

Who are the most important national players in history?

■ *Investigate and write your answer.*

■ *Draw your answer.*

■ *Create and write your personal opinion, comments, variants, etc*

■ *Read and answer the question.*

Who are the most important international players in history?

■ *Investigate and write your answer.*

■ *Draw your answer.*

■ *Create and write your personal opinion, comments, variants, etc*

■ *Read and answer the question.*

Which players have scored the most goals in the history of your country?

■ *Investigate and write your answer.*

■ *Draw your answer.*

■ *Create and write your personal opinion, comments, variants, etc*

Read and answer the question.

Which players have scored the most goals in the history of the world?

Investigate and write your answer.

Draw your answer.

Create and write your personal opinion, comments, variants, etc

■ *Read and answer the question.*

Which players have been named Best Players in the World in the last 10 years?

■ *Investigate and write your answer.*

■ *Draw your answer.*

■ *Create and write your personal opinion, comments, variants, etc*

■ *Read and answer the question.*

What is the best player in your country in your opinion today?

■ *Investigate and write your answer.*

■ *Draw your answer.*

■ *Create and write your personal opinion, comments, variants, etc*

Read and answer the question.

What is the best player in the world in your opinion today?

Investigate and write your answer.

Draw your answer.

Create and write your personal opinion, comments, variants, etc

Read and answer the question.

What is more important for a team, to have a great player or a large block of players? Give reasons for your answer.

Investigate and write your answer.

Draw your answer.

Create and write your personal opinion, comments, variants, etc

■ *Read and answer the question.*

Which players do you think should be given a "fair play" prize?

■ *Investigate and write your answer.*

■ *Draw your answer.*

■ *Create and write your personal opinion, comments, variants, etc*

■ *Read and answer the question.*
....

What is the role of the referees and judges of the game?

■ *Investigate and write your answer.*
....

■ *Draw your answer.*
....

■ *Create and write your personal opinion, comments, variants, etc*
....

■ *Read and answer the question.*

What is the ideal World Selection in all of history?

■ *Investigate and write your answer.*

■ *Draw your answer.*

■ *Create and write your personal opinion, comments, variants, etc*

Read and answer the question.

What is your ideal World Selection today?

Investigate and write your answer.

Draw your answer.

Create and write your personal opinion, comments, variants, etc

■ *Read and answer the question.*

What is the ideal selection of your country in all of history?

■ *Investigate and write your answer.*

■ *Draw your answer.*

■ *Create and write your personal opinion, comments, variants, etc*

■ *Read and answer the question.*

What is your ideal selection of your country today?

■ *Investigate and write your answer.*

■ *Draw your answer.*

■ *Create and write your personal opinion, comments, variants, etc*

■ *Read and answer the question.*

Which are the national teams with the most world titles and your continent in history?

■ *Investigate and write your answer.*

■ *Draw your answer.*

■ *Create and write your personal opinion, comments, variants, etc*

■ *Read and answer the question.*

What have been the best rankings that the selection of your country has achieved in history?

■ *Investigate and write your answer.*

■ *Draw your answer.*

■ *Create and write your personal opinion, comments, variants, etc*

■ *Read and answer the question.*

Which are the most important national clubs in history?

■ *Investigate and write your answer.*

■ *Draw your answer.*

■ *Create and write your personal opinion, comments, variants, etc*

■ *Read and answer the question.*

Which are the most important international clubs in history?

■ *Investigate and write your answer.*

■ *Draw your answer.*

■ *Create and write your personal opinion, comments, variants, etc*

■ *Read and answer the question.*

Summarize the history of your favorite Club.

■ *Investigate and write your answer.*

■ *Draw your answer.*

■ *Create and write your personal opinion, comments, variants, etc*

Read and answer the question.

What is the best classification in the history of your favorite team?

Investigate and write your answer.

Draw your answer.

Create and write your personal opinion, comments, variants, etc

■ *Read and answer the question.*

How is your favorite team's equipment?

■ *Investigate and write your answer.*

■ *Draw your answer.*

■ *Create and write your personal opinion, comments, variants, etc*

■ *Read and answer the question.*

What is your favorite team's stadium like?

■ *Investigate and write your answer.*

■ *Draw your answer.*

■ *Create and write your personal opinion, comments, variants, etc*

■ *Read and answer the question.*

What are the most important national stadiums? What capacity do they have?

■ *Investigate and write your answer.*

■ *Draw your answer.*

■ *Create and write your personal opinion, comments, variants, etc*

Read and answer the question.

Which are the most important international stadiums? What capacity do they have?

Investigate and write your answer.

Draw your answer.

Create and write your personal opinion, comments, variants, etc

■ *Read and answer the question.*

What would you do to improve this sport? What technological innovations do you think could be incorporated into the game to modernize and improve it?

■ *Investigate and write your answer.*

■ *Draw your answer.*

■ *Create and write your personal opinion, comments, variants, etc*

■ *Read and answer the question.*

Do you think this sport is Olympic? Invest it, reason it and give information about it.

■ *Investigate and write your answer.*

■ *Draw your answer.*

■ *Create and write your personal opinion, comments, variants, etc*

■ *Read and answer the question.*

What sports do you think are similar to this one, either because of the elements it uses, or because of its organization or other reasons?

■ *Investigate and write your answer.*

■ *Draw your answer.*

■ *Create and write your personal opinion, comments, variants, etc*

■ *Read and answer the question.*

Invent a similar sport and write the characteristics of it.

■ *Investigate and write your answer.*

■ *Draw your answer.*

■ *Create and write your personal opinion, comments, variants, etc*

■ *Read and answer the question.*

What are the organizations and federations that organize this sport in your country and in the world?

■ *Investigate and write your answer.*

■ *Draw your answer.*

■ *Create and write your personal opinion, comments, variants, etc*

CPSIA information can be obtained
at www.ICGtesting.com
Printed in the USA
BVHW011135180721
612259BV00022B/477

9 781981 872466